Kindergarten Puzzles

Level 1

Simple Puzzles, Worksheets, and Activities for Kids

written by

Peter I. Kattan
and
Nicola I. Kattan

PETRA BOOKS
www.KindergartenSudoku.com

Kindergarten Puzzles – Level 1
Simple Puzzles, Worksheets, and Activities for Kids
by Peter I. Kattan and Nicola I. Kattan

The various images appearing in this book were purchased from the Fotolia website at www.fotolia.com . Consequently, the respective authors of these images grant us the right to use these images in this publication royalty free while they retain the copyrights for their work. Thus, we would like to acknowledge their contribution here. The dog and cat images are © Bello from Brazil, the hen image is © Ewe Degiampietro from Germany, the goat image is © piumadaquila from Italy, the bear image is © Alexey Bannykh from Russia, the fax and printer images are © Kamran Akhlag from Pakistan, the computer image is © Elena Svedenco from Moldova, the book image is © Actomic from Germany, and the mouse image is © algabafoto from Spain.

The authors would like to thank Roger White for designing the fonts NationalFirstFontDotted and NationalFirstFont and making them available in the public domain. These fonts are used on some selected pages of this book. His website address is http://www.rogersfonts.org.uk

Contents

Contents (Continued)

Join Similar Words of Animals

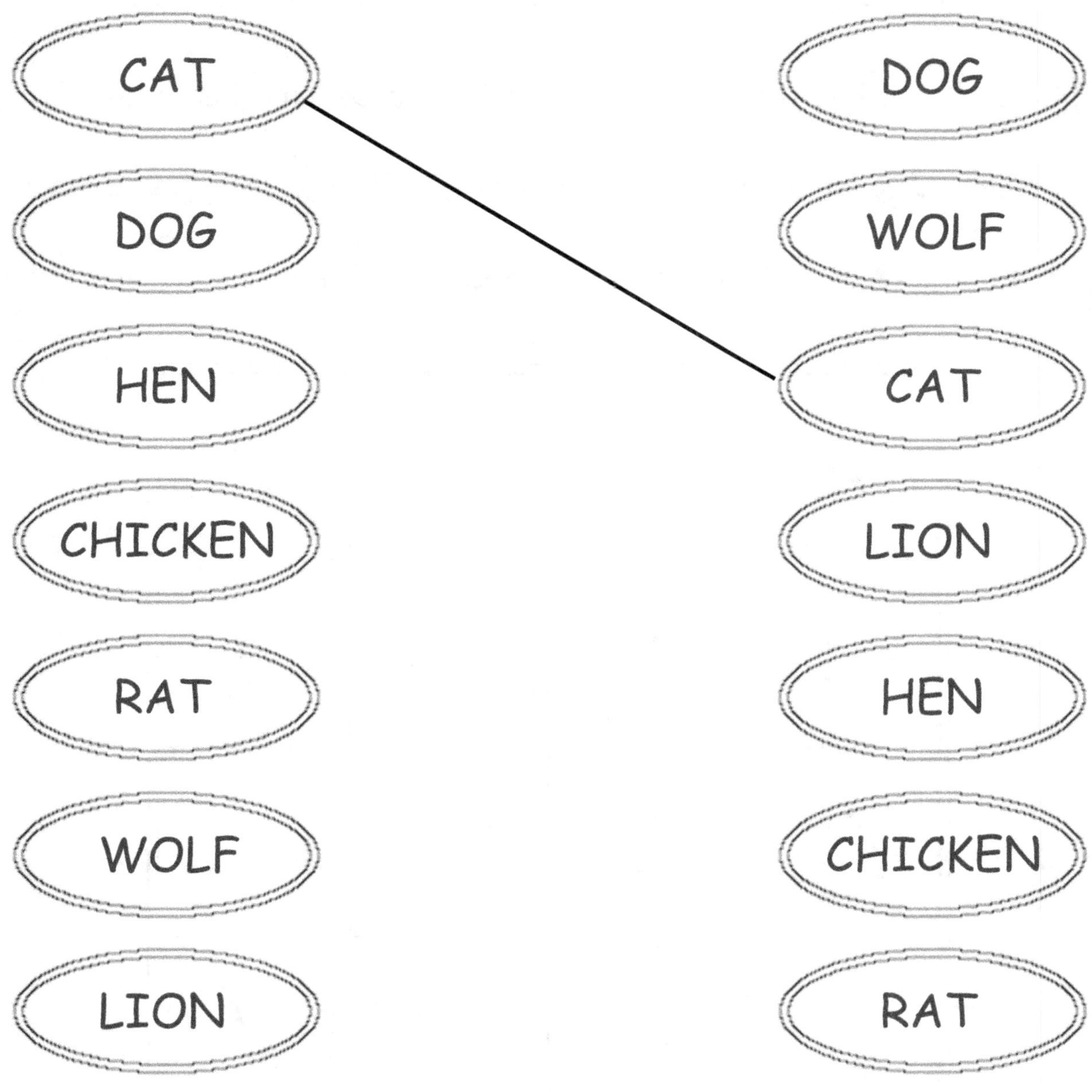

Sudoku
Fill the blanks with the numbers 1,2,3,4 such that

01   Each row has the four numbers 1,2,3,4 appearing just once.

02   Each Column has the four numbers 1,2,3,4 appearing just once.

03   Each 2x2 block has the four numbers 1,2,3,4 appearing just once.

4			2
2	1		4
3	2	4	
	4		3

Count the Animals

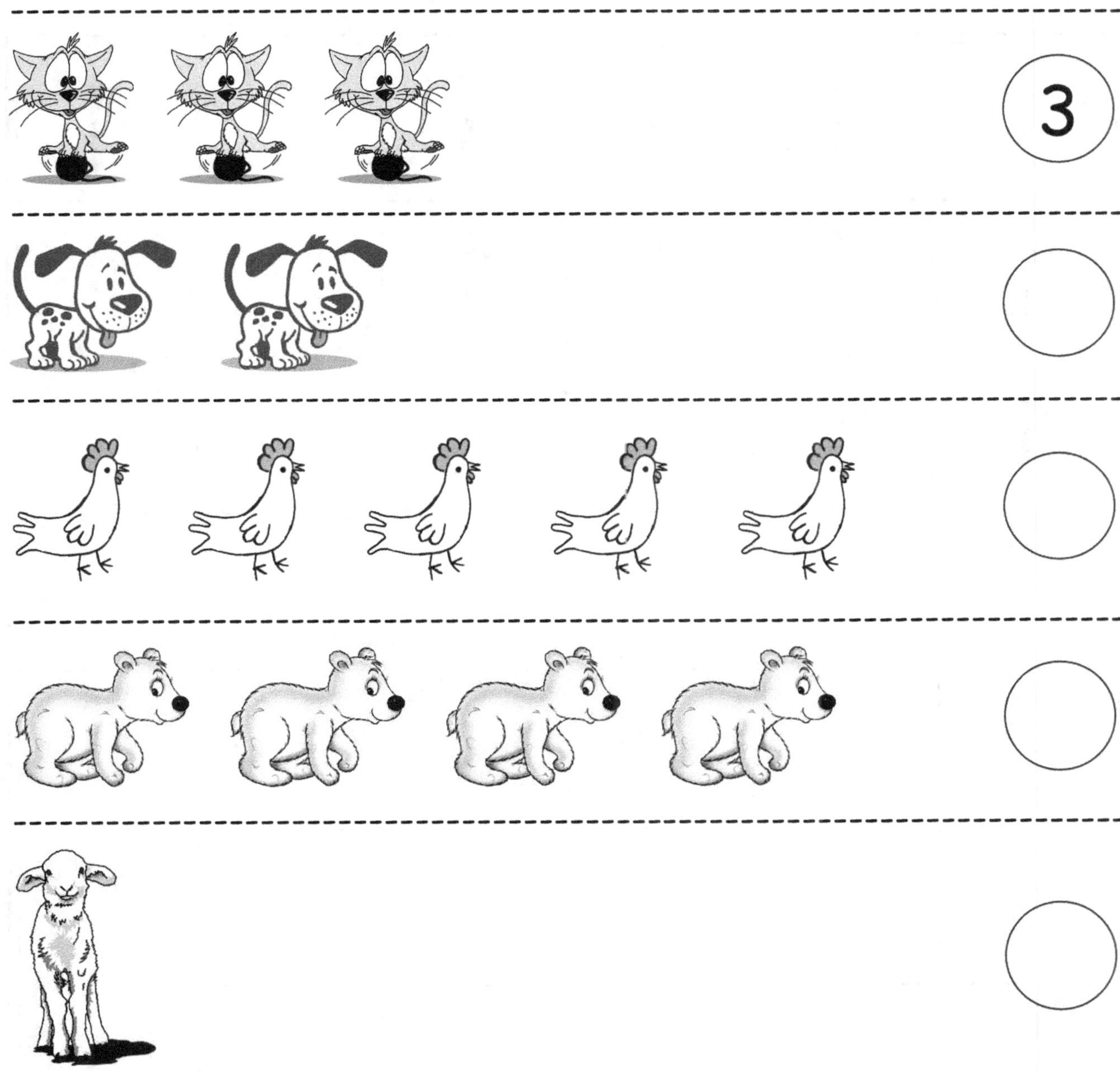

Trace this Number

1	1	1	1	1	1
1	1	1	1		
1	1				

Coloring

Color the dog yellow

Color the chicken red

Circle What Comes Next?

Sudoku
Fill the blanks with the numbers 1,2,3,4 such that

01 Each row has the four numbers 1,2,3,4 appearing just once.

02 Each Column has the four numbers 1,2,3,4 appearing just once.

03 Each 2x2 block has the four numbers 1,2,3,4 appearing just once.

2			4
3		1	
	2	4	3
4	3		1

Count then Choose the Correct Number

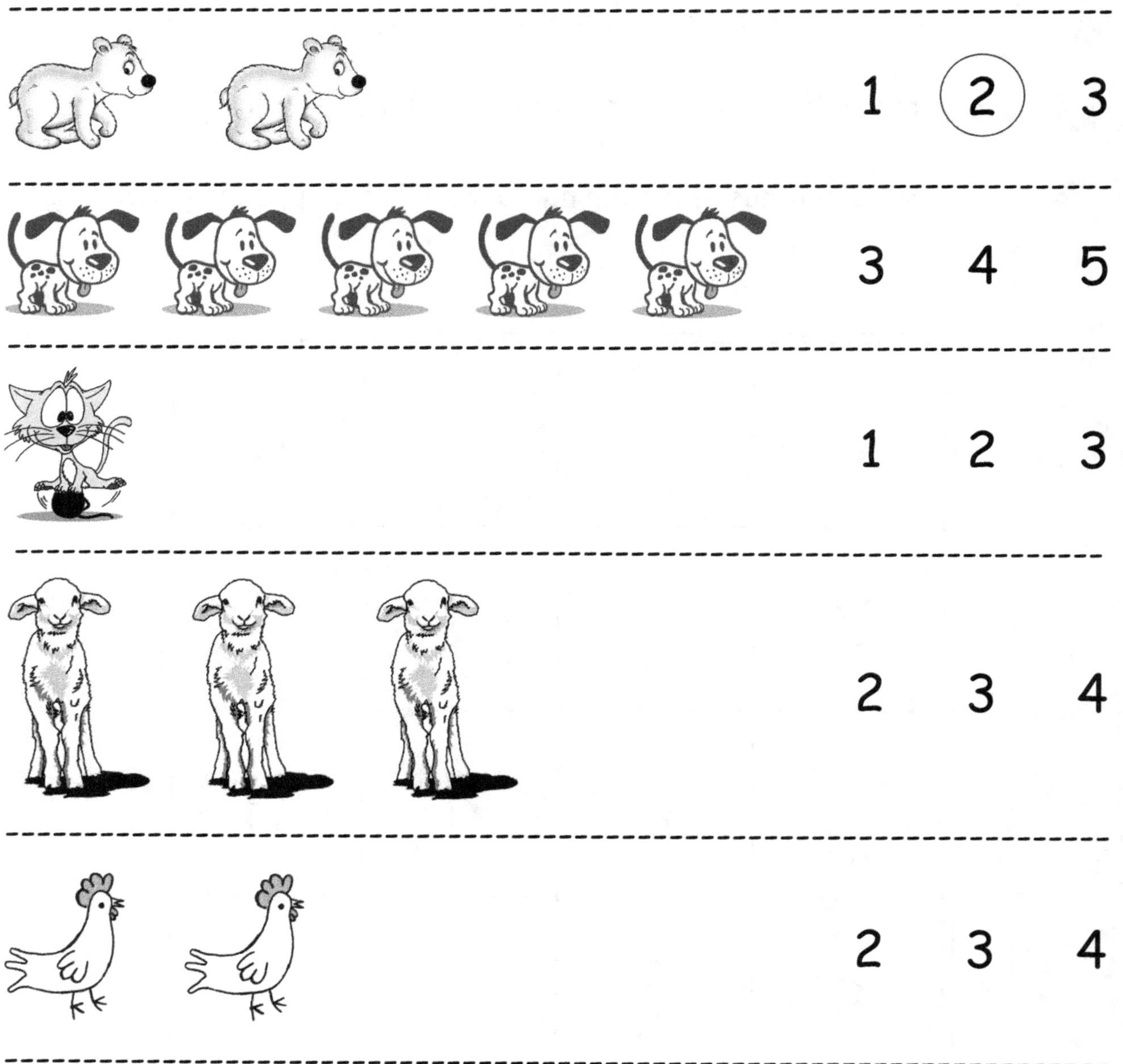

	1	(2)	3
	3	4	5
	1	2	3
	2	3	4
	2	3	4

Maze

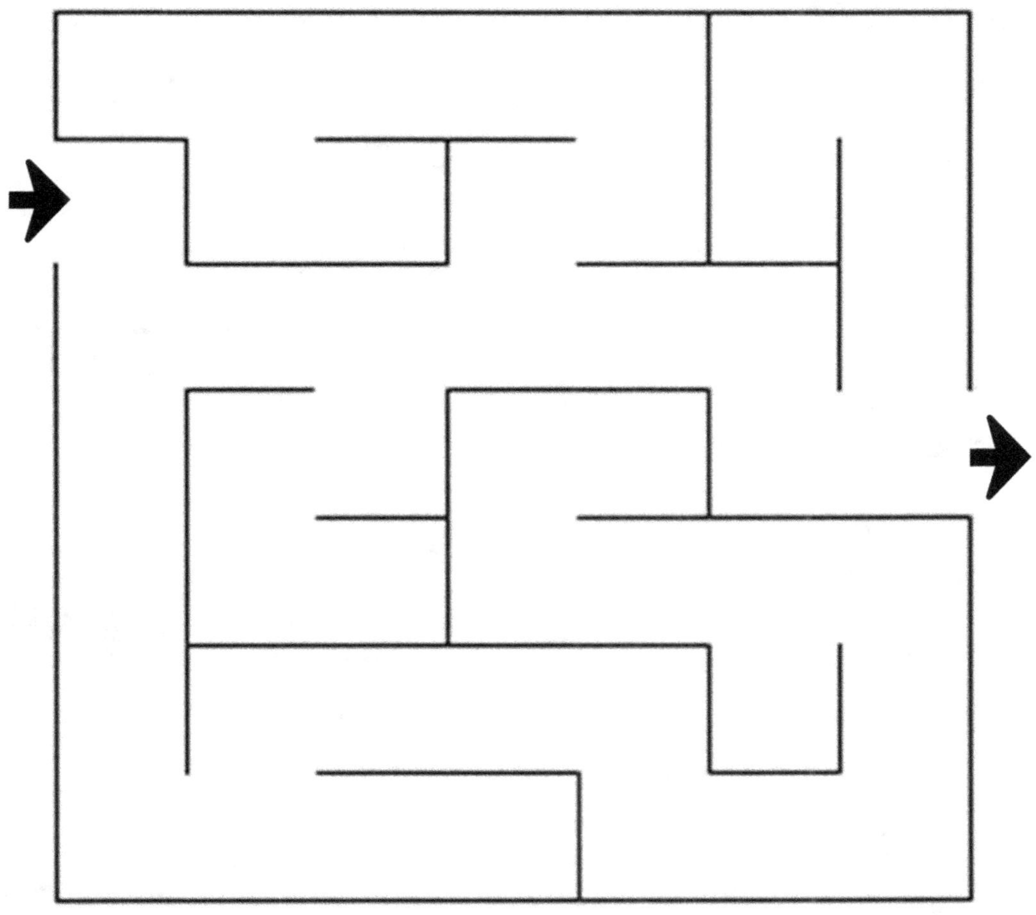

Name the Animals

Circle the Different Animal

Sudoku
Fill the blanks with the numbers 1,2,3,4 such that

01 Each row has the four numbers 1,2,3,4 appearing just once.

02 Each Column has the four numbers 1,2,3,4 appearing just once.

03 Each 2x2 block has the four numbers 1,2,3,4 appearing just once.

4	3		2
		3	
1		2	3
	2	4	1

Trace these Letters

A   A   A   A   A

B   B   B   B   B

C   C   C   C   C

D   D   D   D   D

E   E   E   E   E

Trace these Shapes

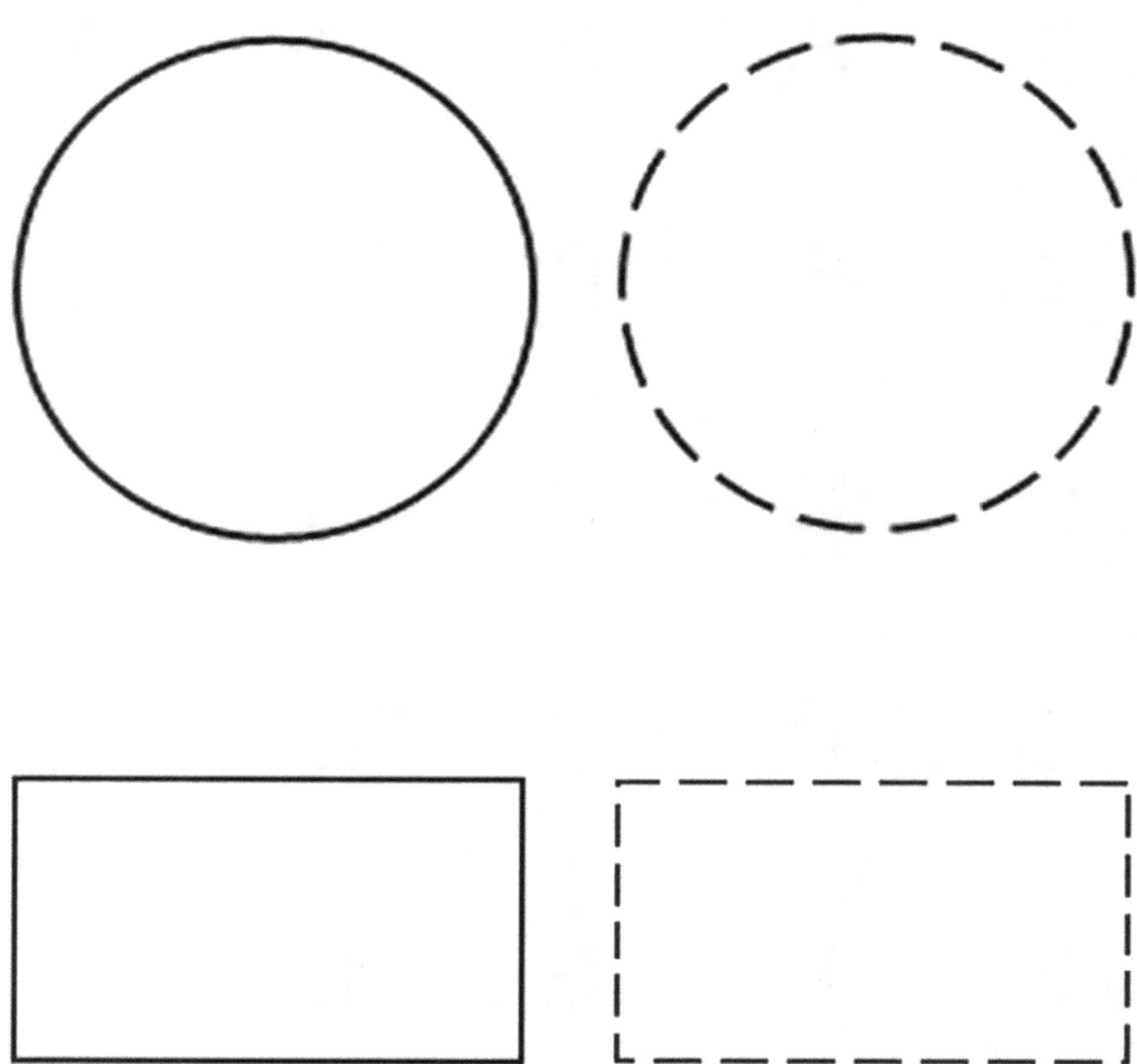

Fill the Missing Letters

Join Similar Words of Things

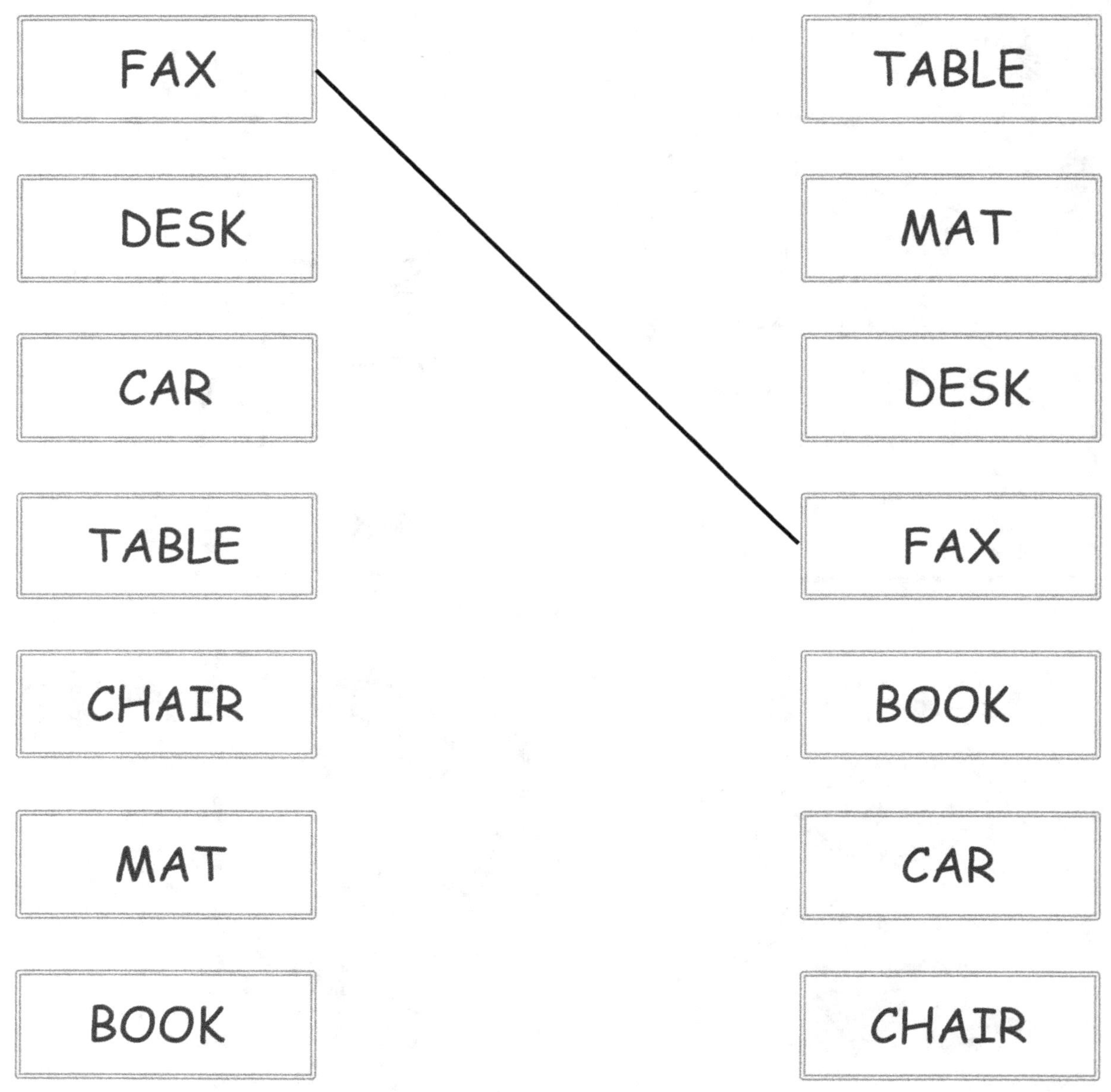

Count these Things

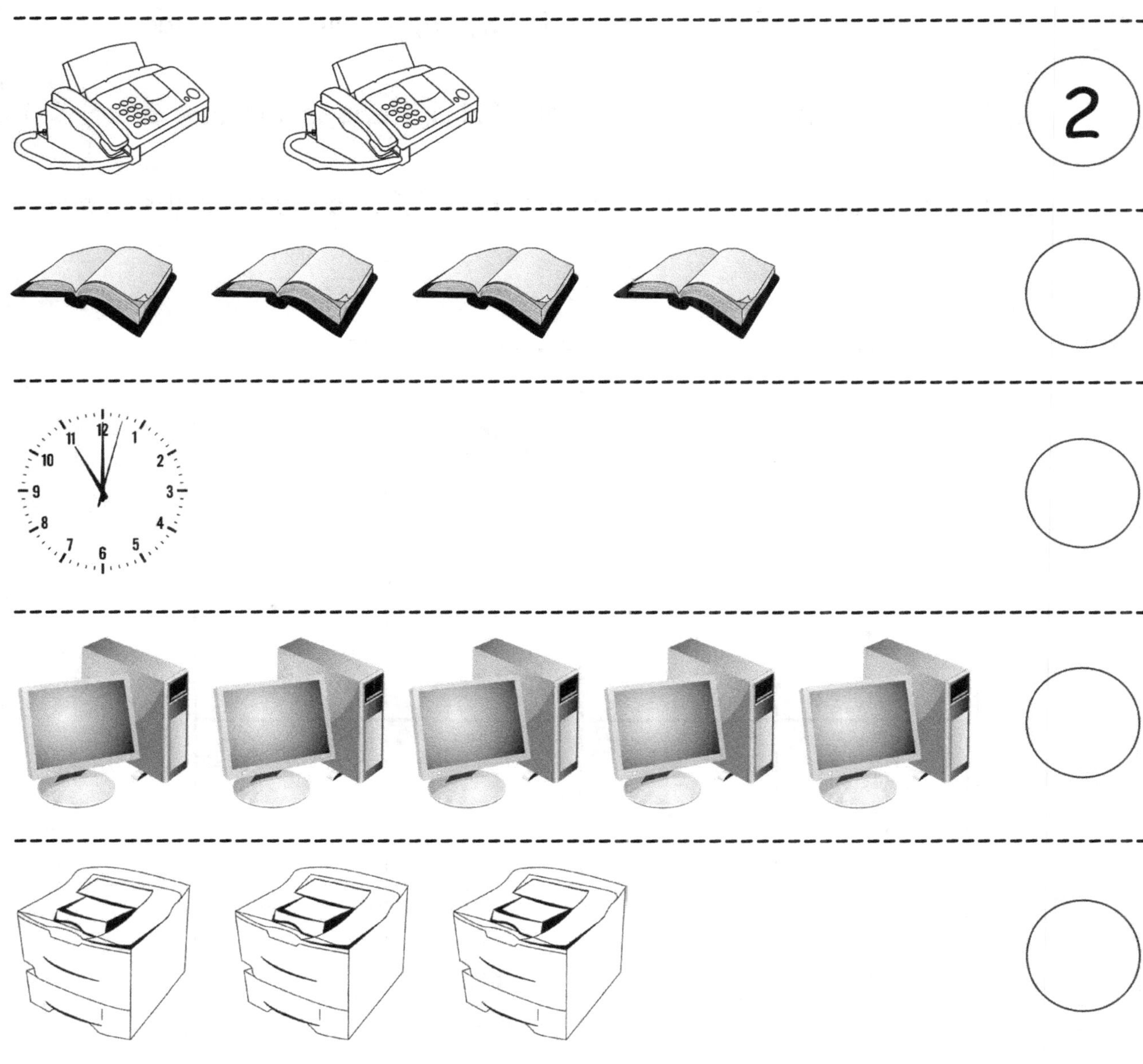

Sudoku

Fill the blanks with the numbers 1,2,3,4 such that

01 Each row has the four numbers 1,2,3,4 appearing just once.

02 Each Column has the four numbers 1,2,3,4 appearing just once.

03 Each 2x2 block has the four numbers 1,2,3,4 appearing just once.

		4	1
1	4		2
3	2		
4		2	3

Trace these Letters

F   F   F   F   F

G   G   G   G   G

H   H   H   H   H

I   I   I   I   I

J   J   J   J   J

Maze

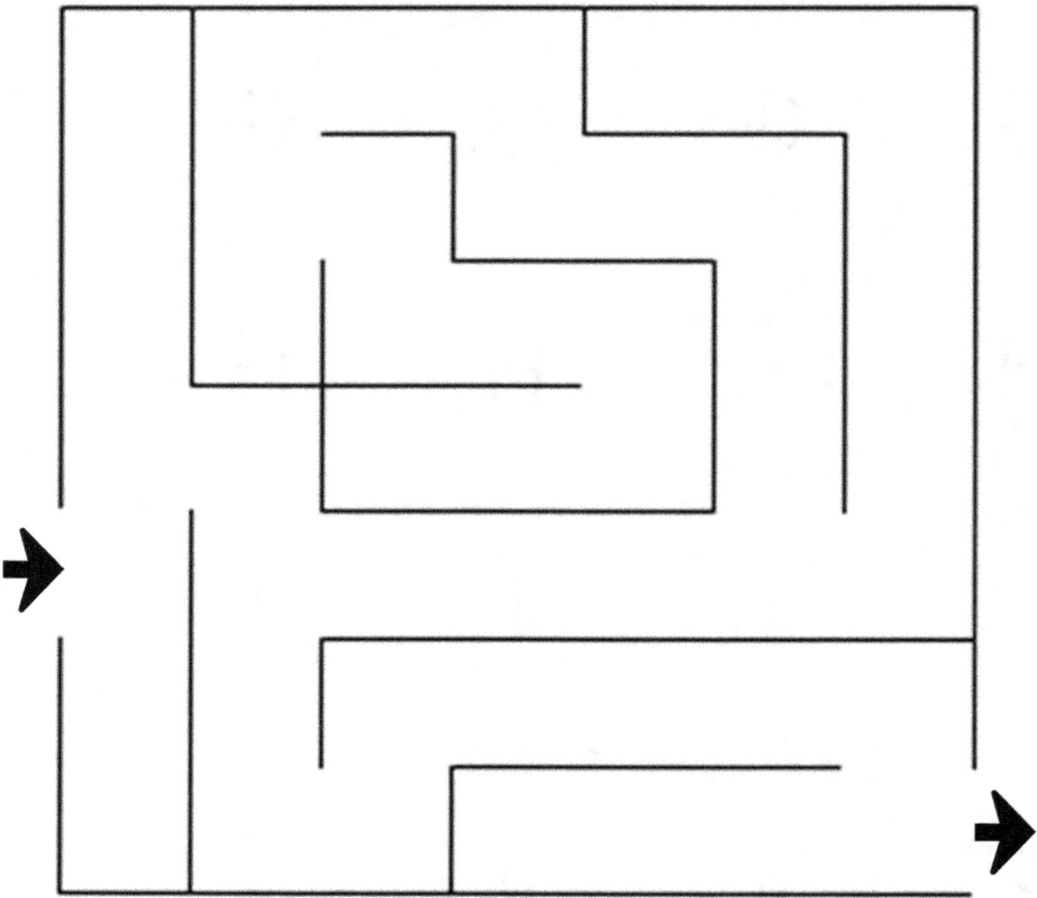

Trace this Number

2	2	2	2	2	2
2	2	2	2		
2	2				

Tic Tac Toe

Fill the blanks with O or X

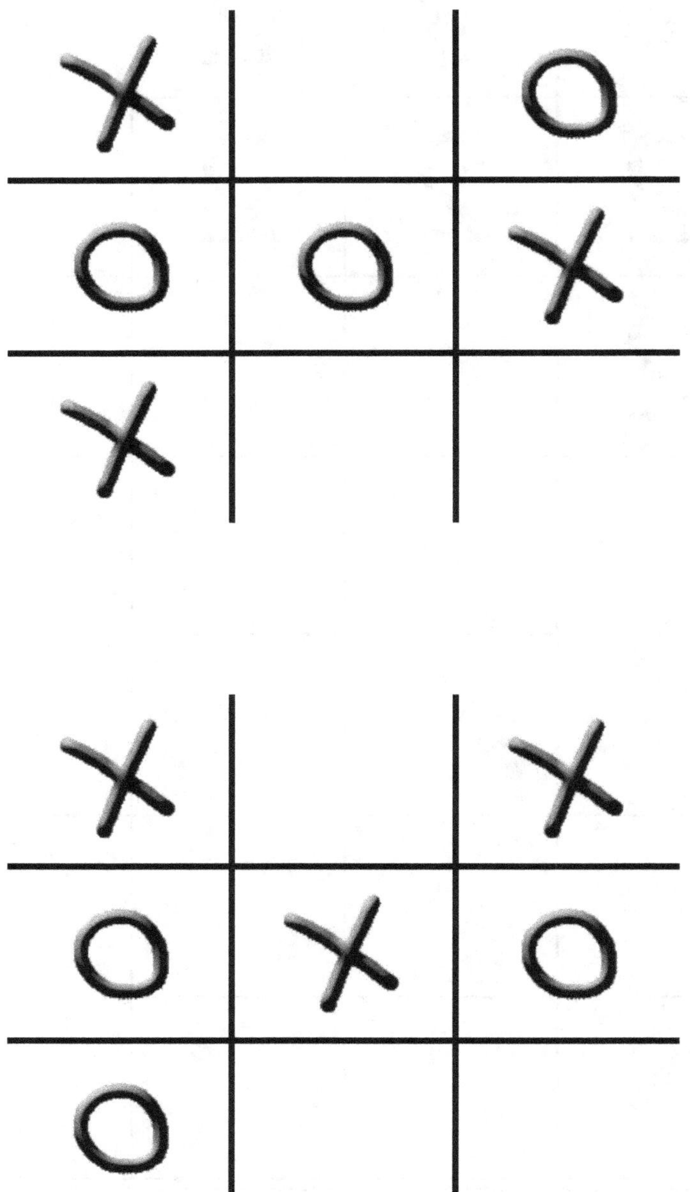

Draw as Many Shapes as Needed

		4
○		3
△		2
☆		1
◇		5

Circle the Different Thing

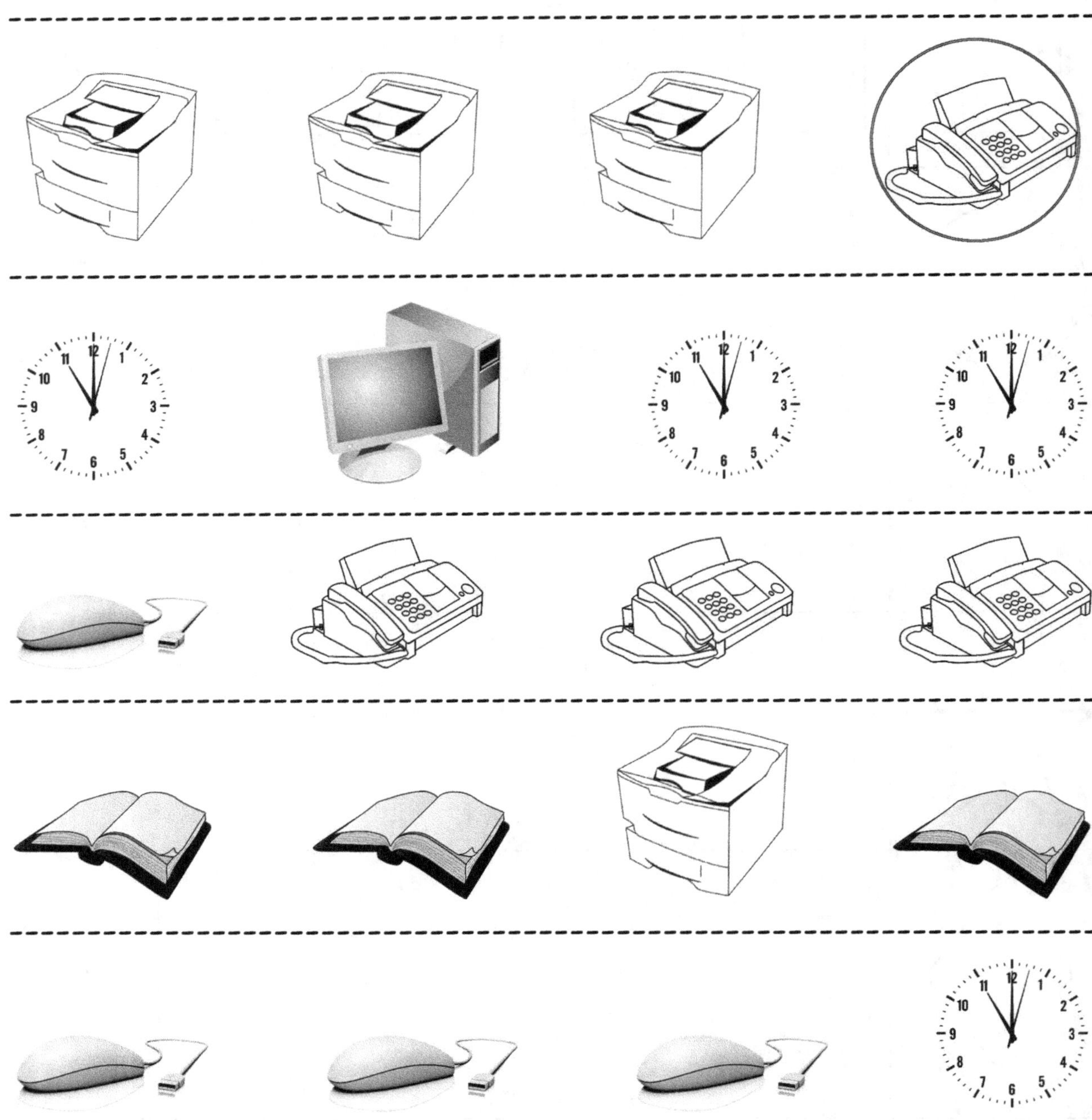

What are the Missing Numbers ?

1		3		5

	2		4	5

1	2		4	

1		3	4	

Sudoku
Fill the blanks with the numbers 1,2,3,4 such that

01 Each row has the four numbers 1,2,3,4 appearing just once.

02 Each Column has the four numbers 1,2,3,4 appearing just once.

03 Each 2x2 block has the four numbers 1,2,3,4 appearing just once.

3	1		
	2	3	1
1		4	2
	4		3

Maze

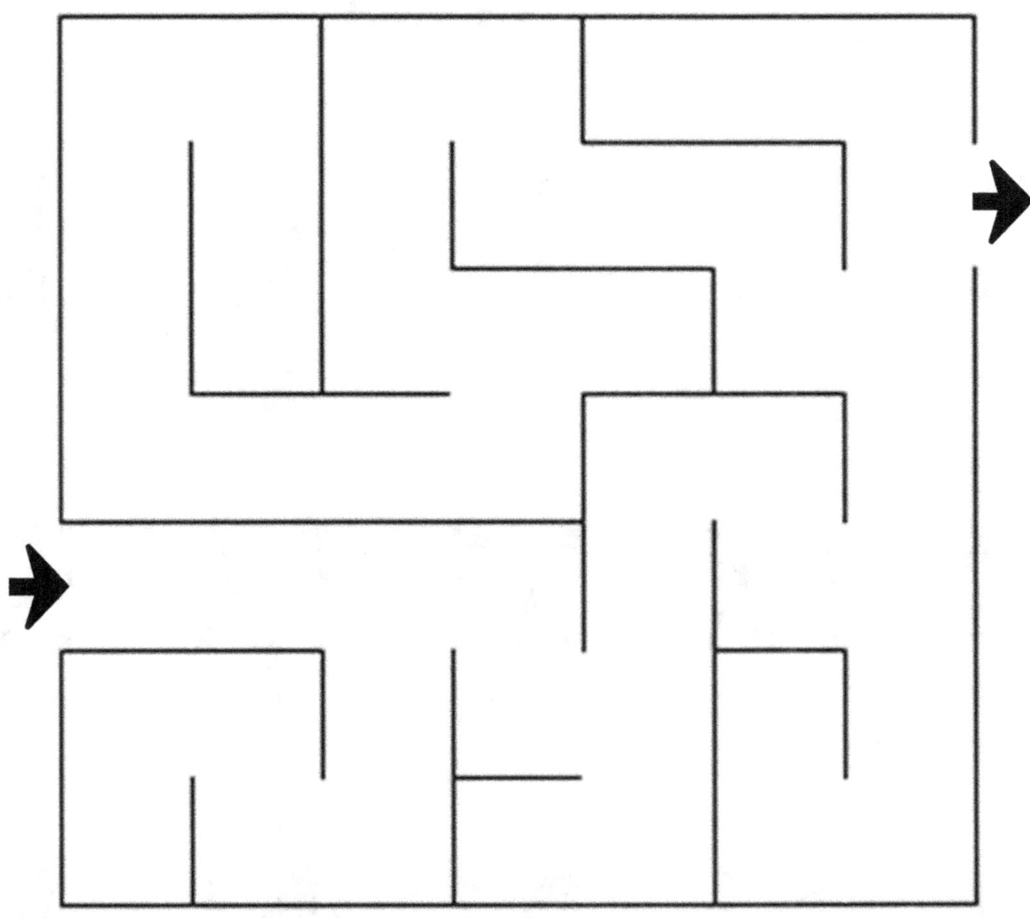

Trace these Letters

K K K K K

L L L L L

M M M M M

N N N N N

Find and Circle the Number 1

1	0	2	1	3	1	4
2	5	4	1	0	2	1
1	1	2	3	2	1	0

Find and Circle the Number 2

1	2	0	3	2	4	1
2	1	5	4	3	2	2
1	0	2	4	1	2	3

Find and Circle the Number 3

1	3	2	3	3	4	1
0	1	2	2	3	4	3
3	2	1	3	2	0	1

Circle the Object Does not Fit Below

Trace these Shapes

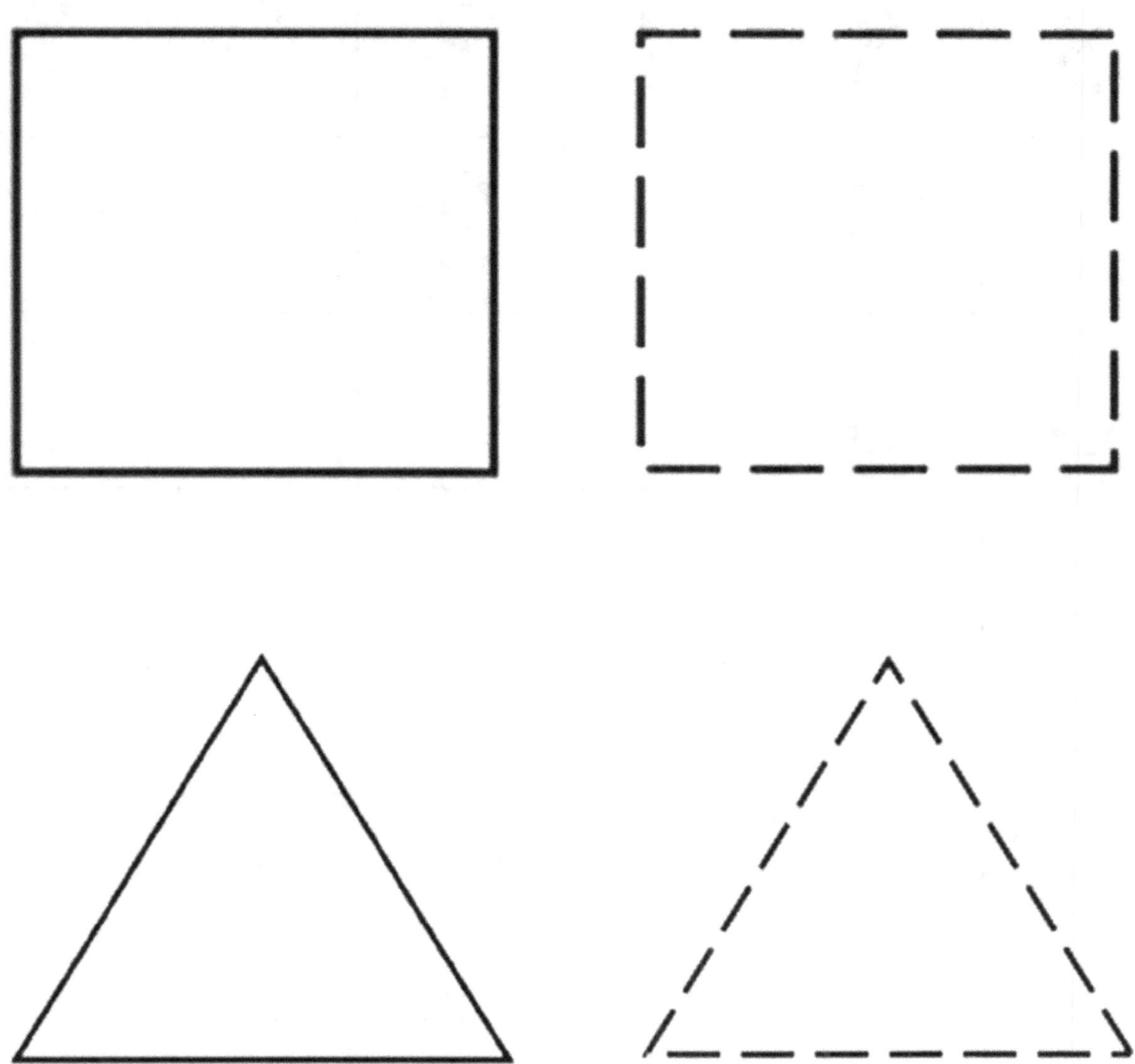

Trace this Number

3	3	3	3	3	3
3	3	3	3		
3	3				

Maze

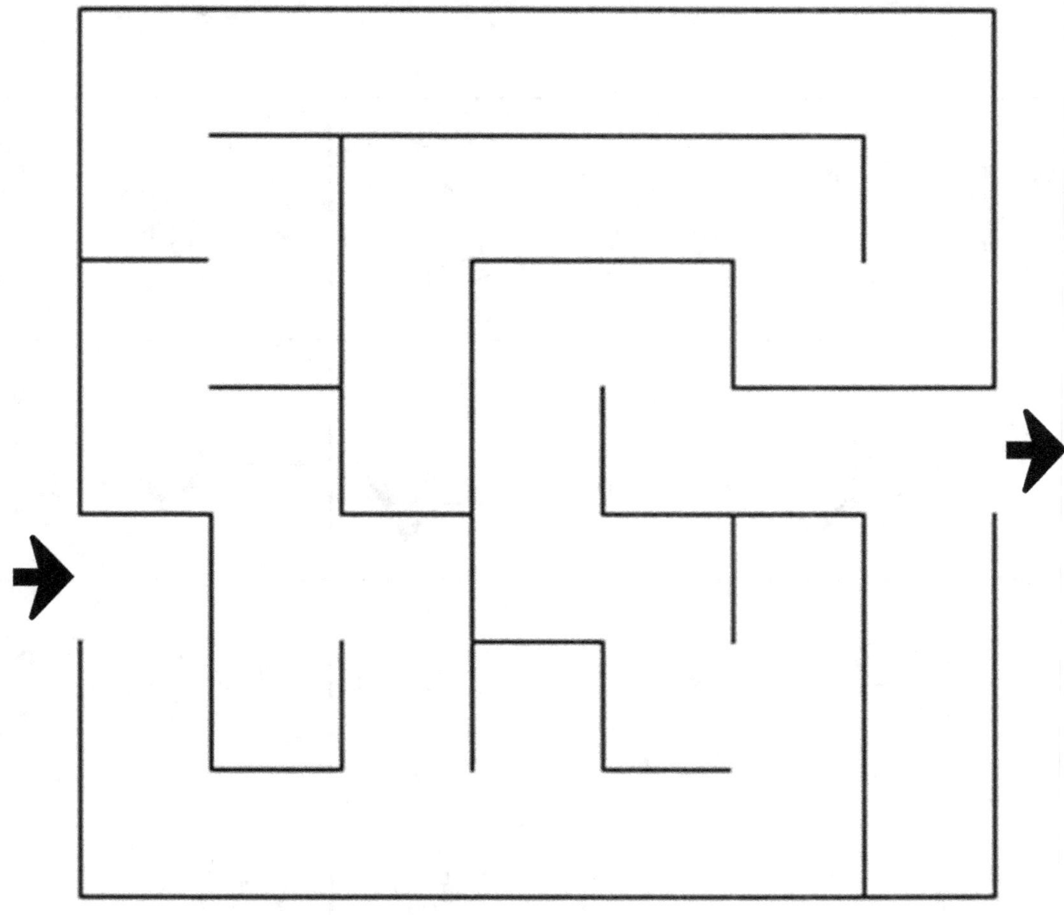

Circle What Comes Next?

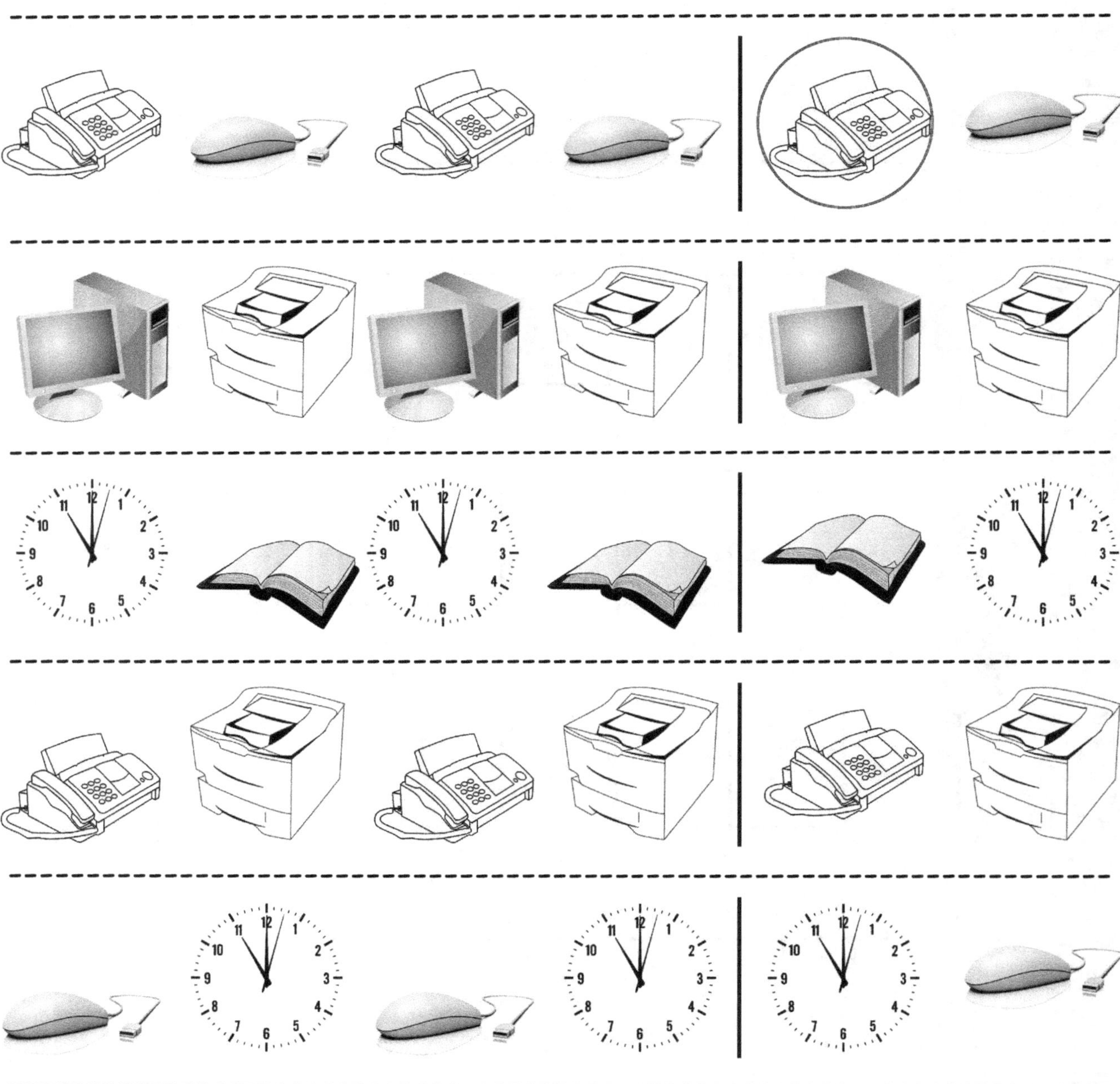

The Dog Wants to Go Around the Numbers
Draw a Line for its Journey

Count then Choose the Correct Number

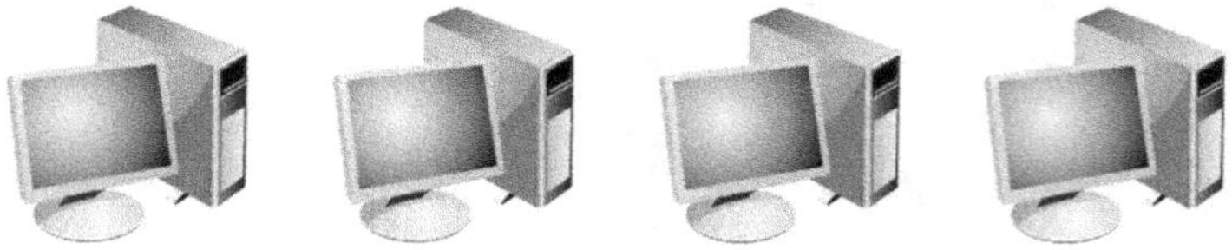

2   (4)   3

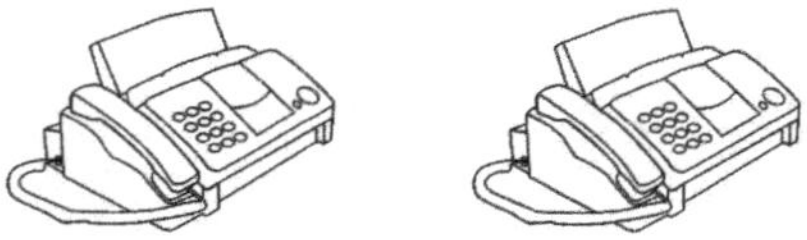

3   1   2

3   4   5

1   3   2

1   2   3

2   1   3

Circle the Different Shape

Coloring

Color the bear blue

Color the goat green

Count then Choose the Correct Number

1   (2)   3

3   4   5

1   2   3

3   4   5

2   1   3

Maze

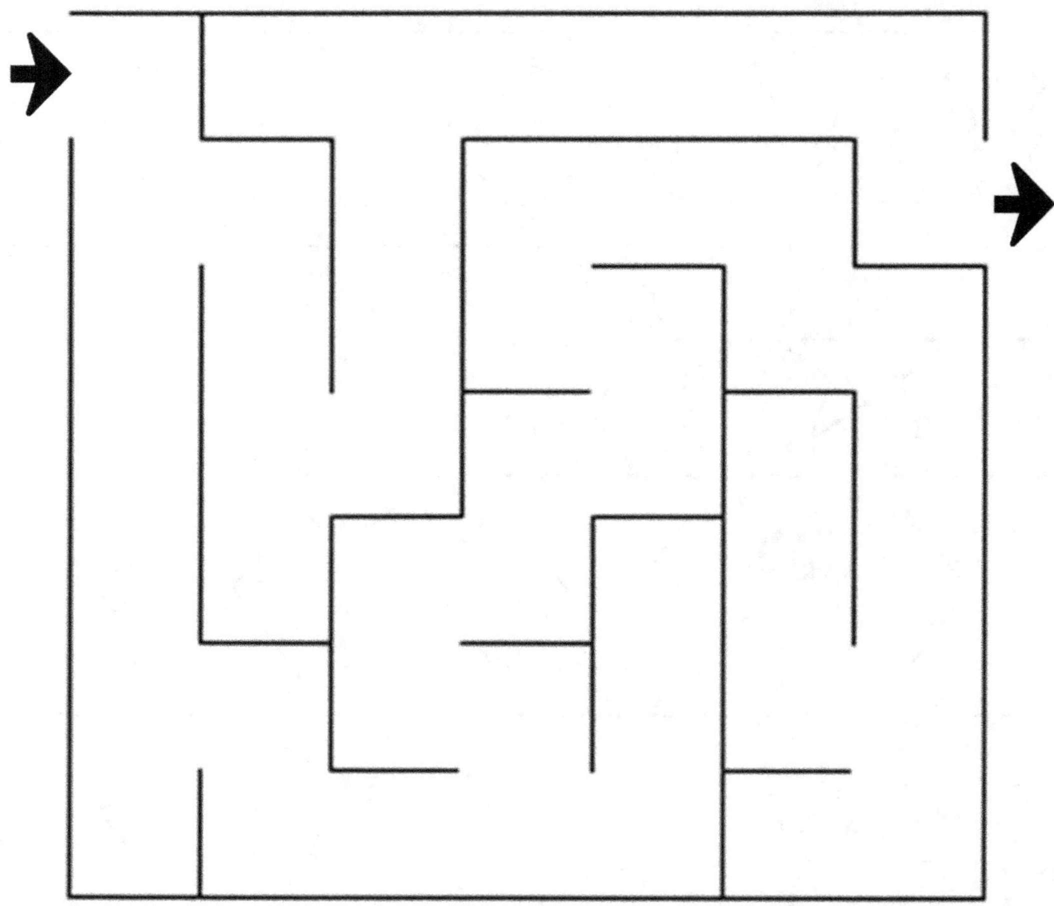

Count these Shapes

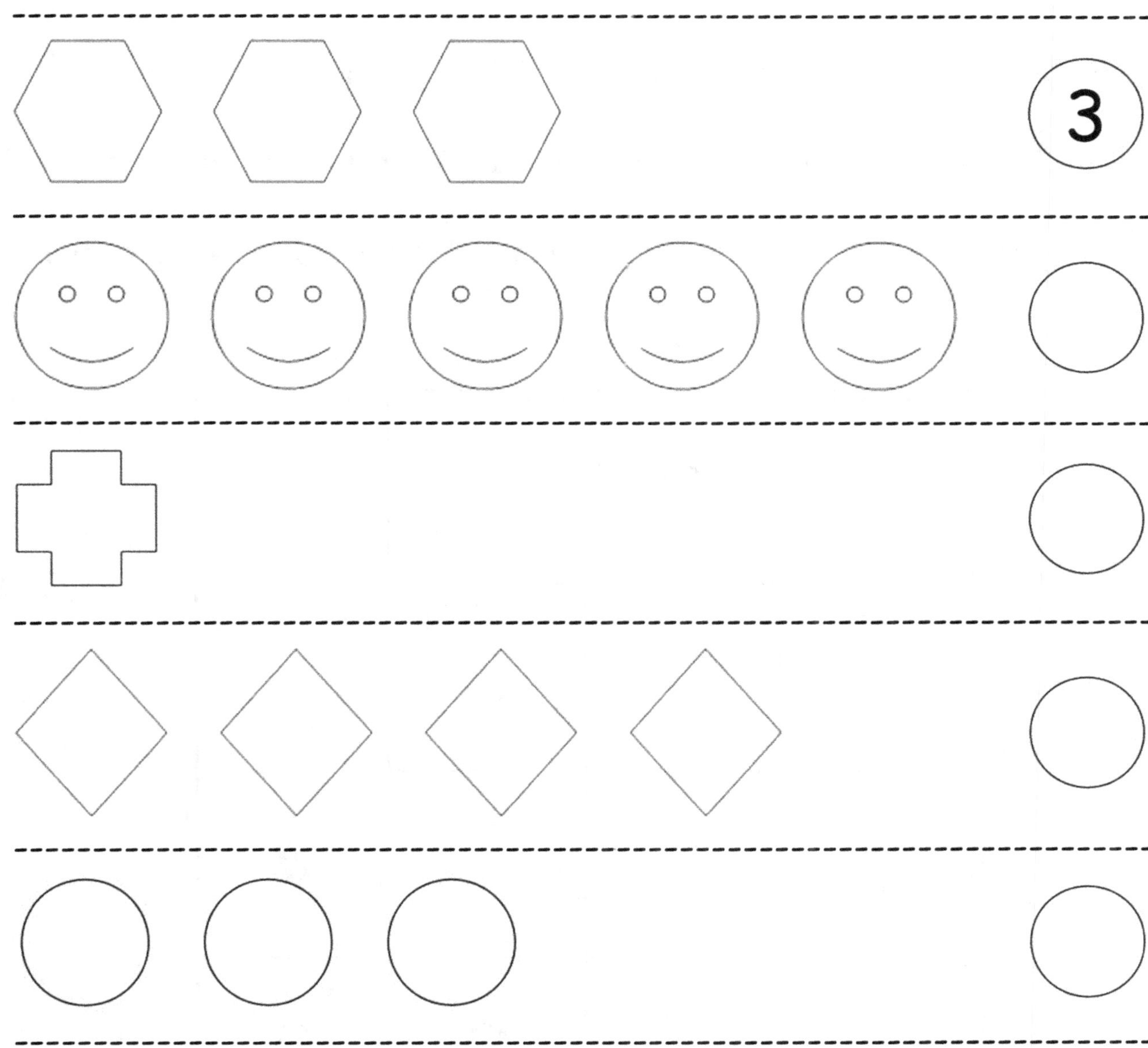

Sudoku
Fill the blanks with the numbers 1,2,3,4 such that

01 Each row has the four numbers 1,2,3,4 appearing just once.

02 Each Column has the four numbers 1,2,3,4 appearing just once.

03 Each 2x2 block has the four numbers 1,2,3,4 appearing just once.

3	2		1
		3	
2	3		4
	4	2	3

Trace this Number

4	4	4	4	4	4
4	4	4	4		
4	4				

Join the Days of the Week

MONDAY	WEDNESDAY
TUESDAY	SATURDAY
WEDNESDAY	FRIDAY
THURSDAY	SUNDAY
FRIDAY	MONDAY
SATURDAY	TUESDAY
SUNDAY	THURSDAY

Name these Things

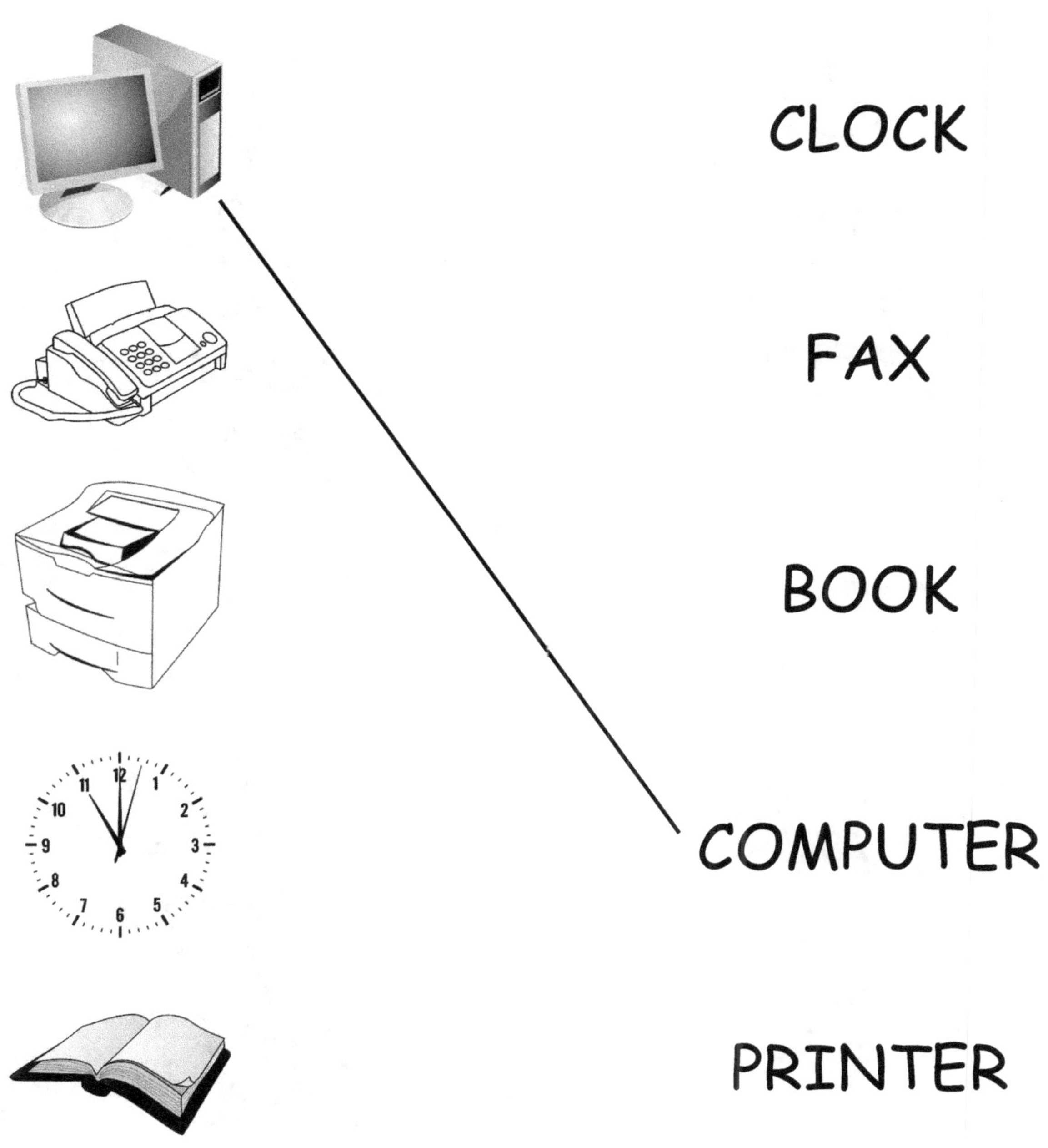

CLOCK

FAX

BOOK

COMPUTER

PRINTER

Count the Steps

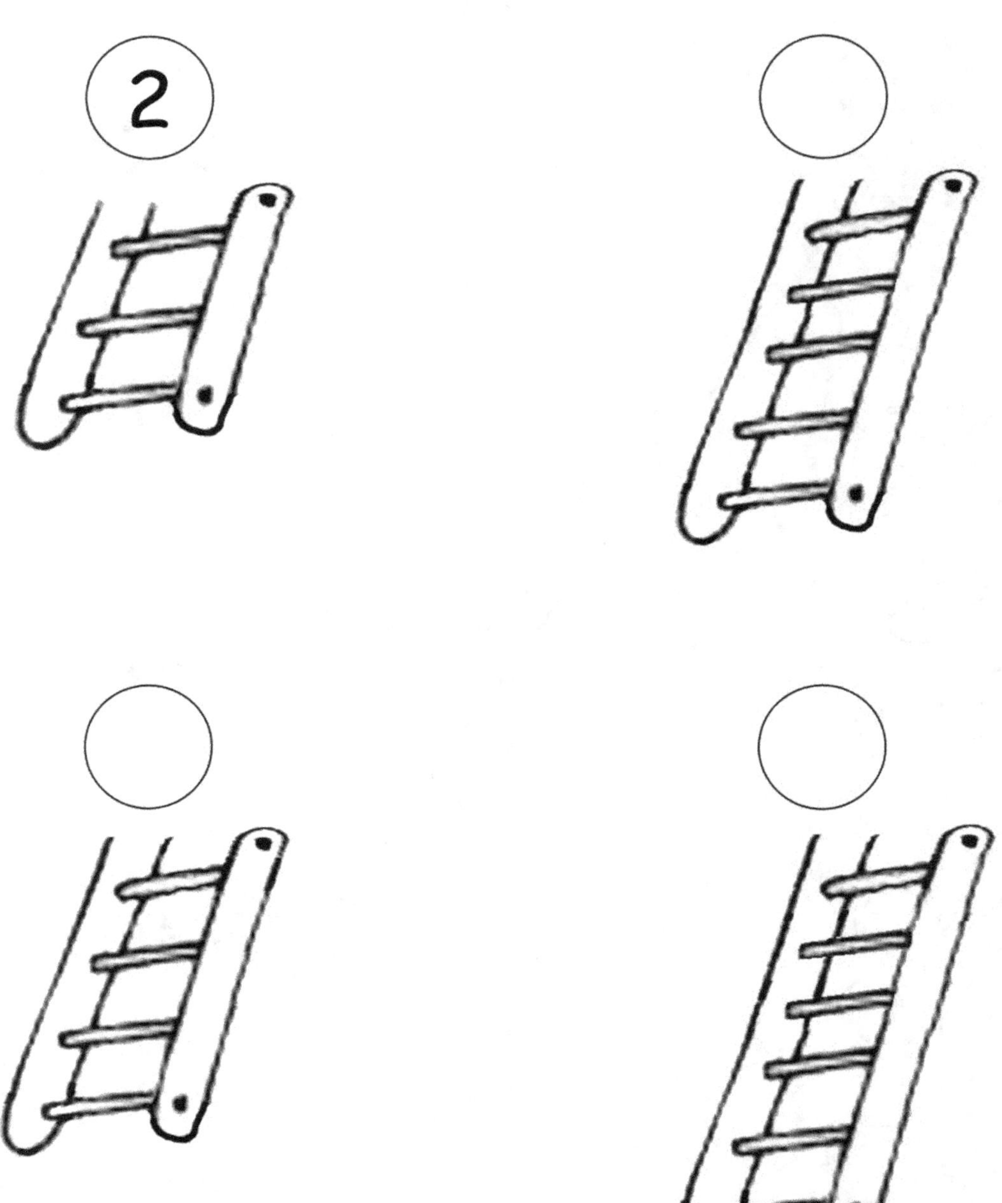

Fill the Missing Letters

Circle the Object that Does not Fit Below

Maze

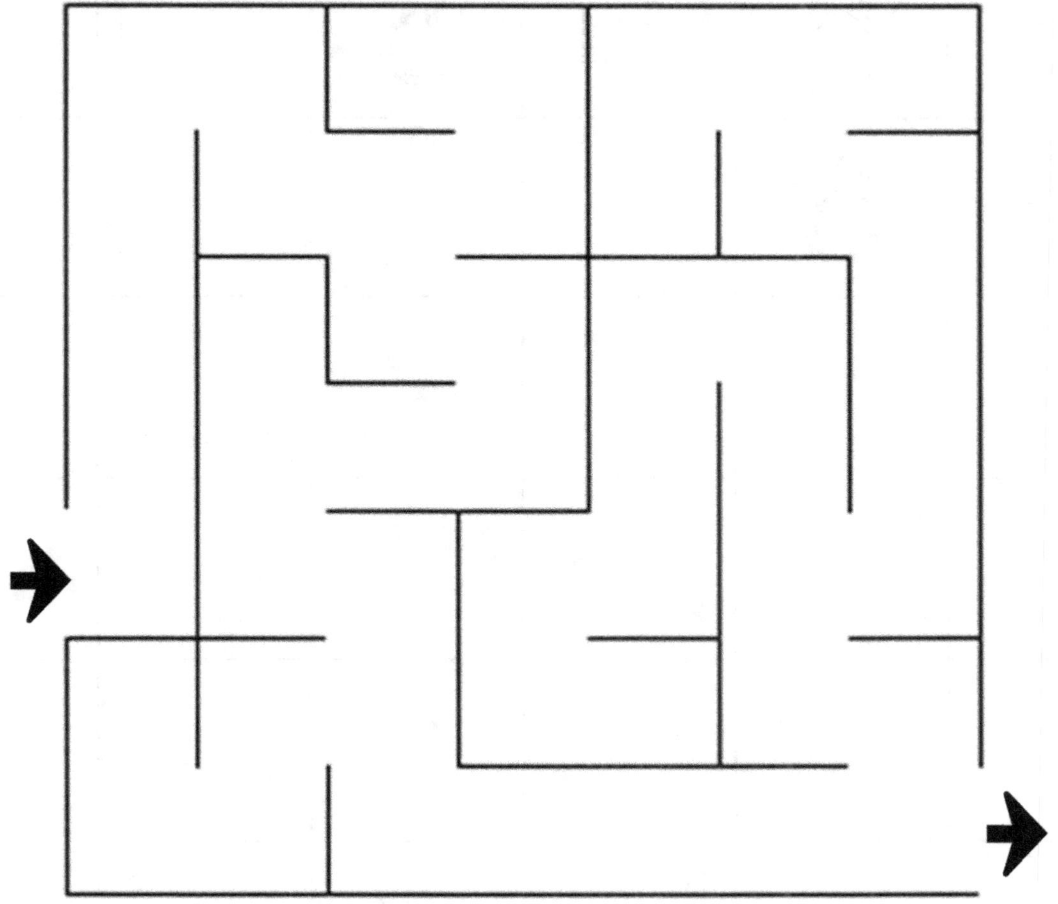

Trace this Number

5	5	5	5	5	5
5	5	5	5		
5	5				

Arrows and Directions

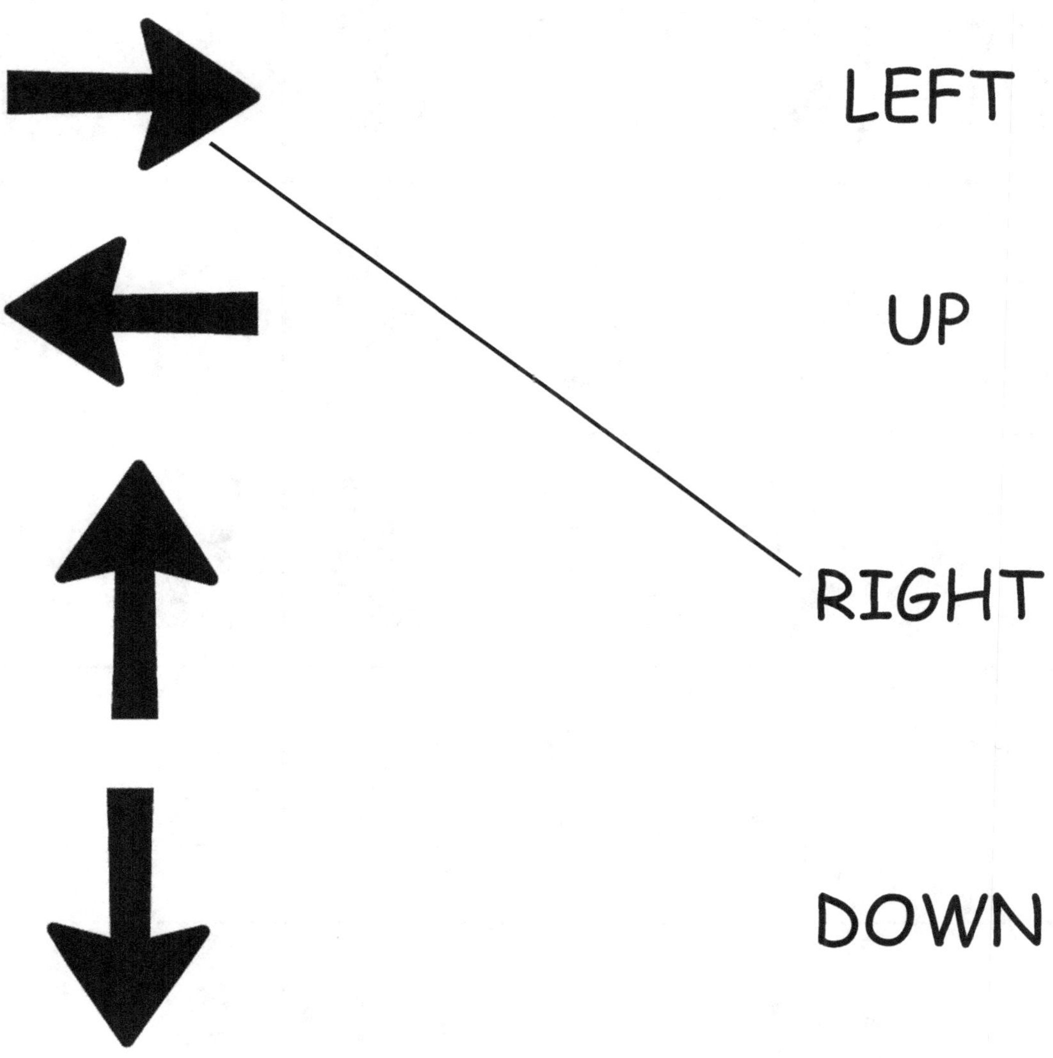

Circle What Comes Next?

Trace these Numbers

1   1   1   1   1

2   2   2   2   2

3   3   3   3   3

4   4   4   4   4

5   5   5   5   5

Color each Shape

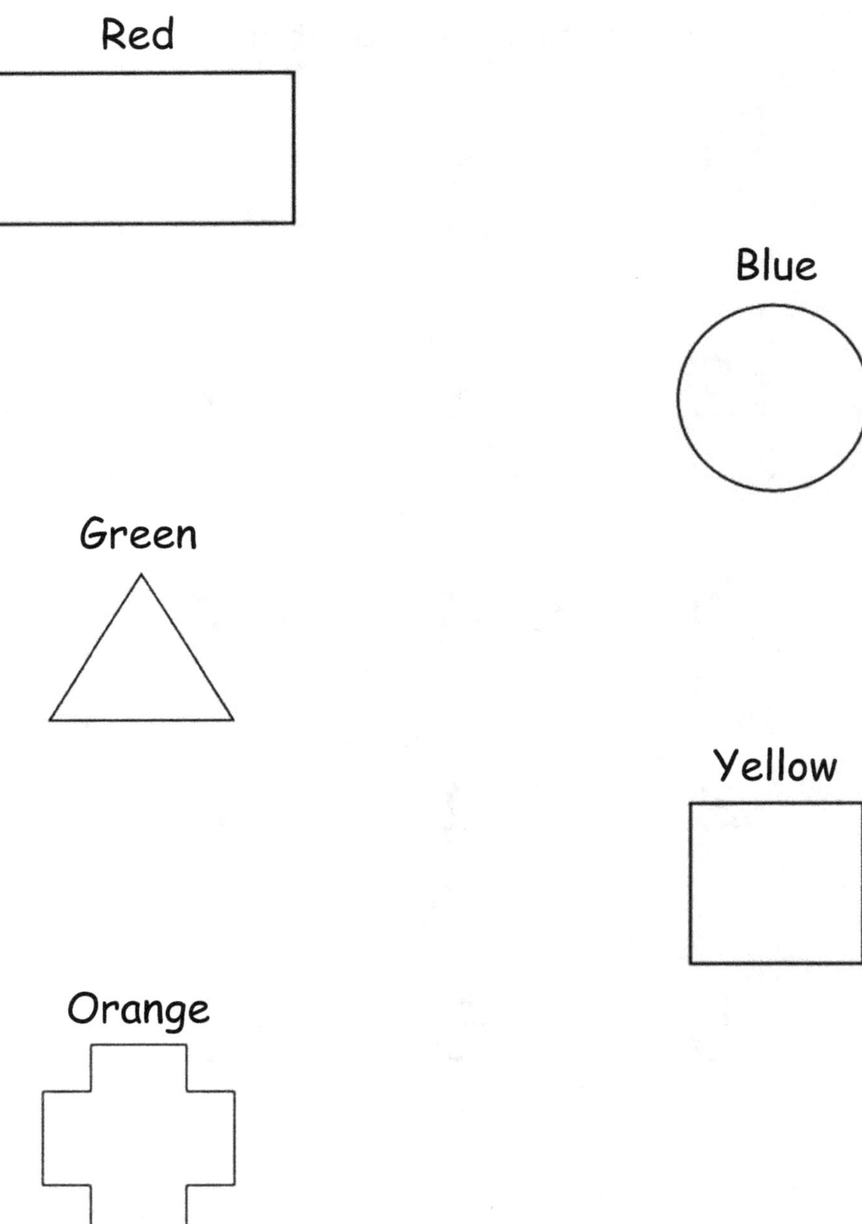

Find and Circle the Number 4

1	2	4	3	4	1	0
4	2	1	3	1	2	4
4	1	2	4	4	1	3
1	4	2	3	0	5	3

Find and Circle the Number 5

5	2	2	3	1	0	4
1	5	2	5	3	2	5
2	3	3	5	4	1	2
5	5	2	1	3	5	0

Sudoku
Fill the blanks with the numbers 1,2,3,4 such that

01 Each row has the four numbers 1,2,3,4 appearing just once.

02 Each Column has the four numbers 1,2,3,4 appearing just once.

03 Each 2x2 block has the four numbers 1,2,3,4 appearing just once.

			3
4	3	2	
3	4		2
	1	3	4

Maze

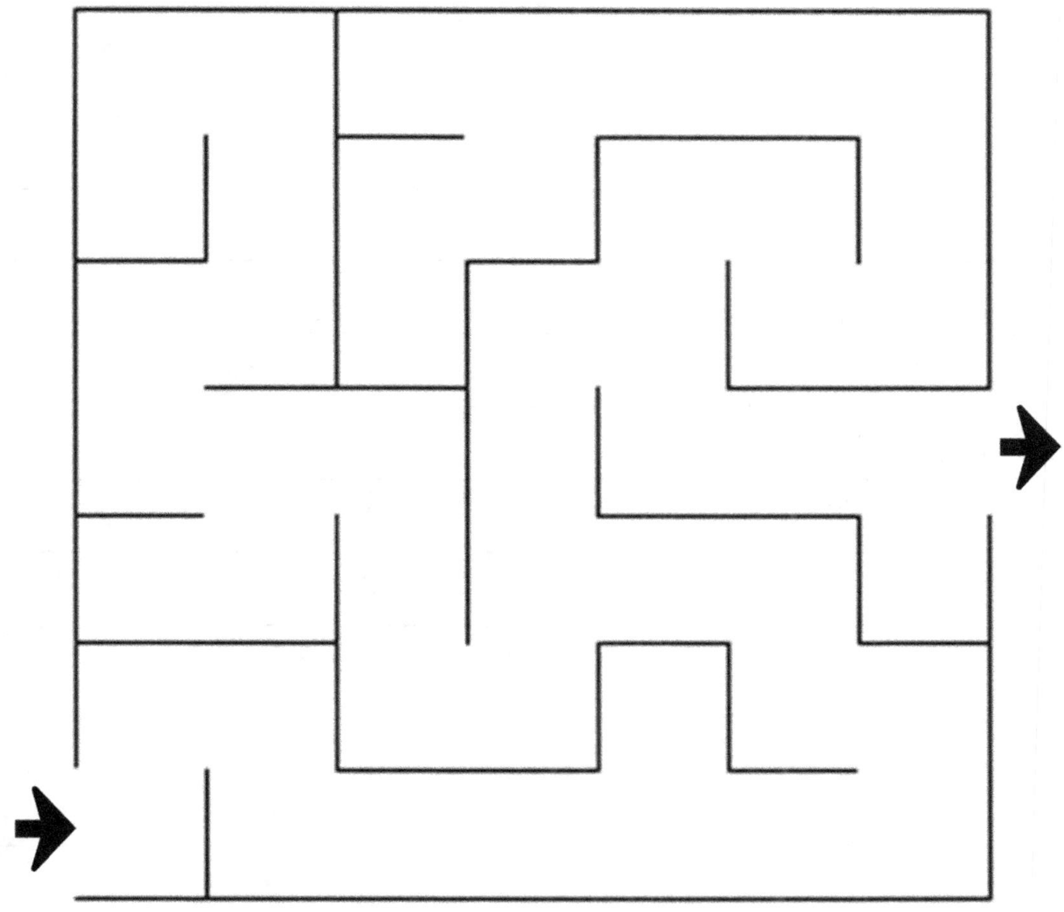

Name:

Age:

Notes

Kindergarten Puzzles – Level 2
Simple Puzzles, Worksheets, and Activities for Kids

Check the companion book containing Level 2 puzzles that include mazes, Sudoku, Kakuro, counting, shape puzzles, letter puzzles, and simple addition and subtraction.

Also Available by the Same Authors:

Kindergarten Sudoku
4x4 Sudoku Puzzles for Kids

More Kindergarten Sudoku
4x4 Classic Sudoku Puzzles for Kids

The Big Book of Kindergarten Sudoku
4x4 Sudoku Puzzles for Kids

Beyond Kindergarten Sudoku
6x6 Sudoku Puzzles for Kids

THE BIG BOOK OF
KINDERGARTEN
SUDOKU
1
1 2
1
2 4
200 Puzzles Included
4x4 Sudoku Puzzles for Kids
Peter I. Kattan
Nicola I. Kattan

Beyond Kindergarten
Sudoku
6x6 Sudoku Puzzles for Kids
1
1 5 6 3
3 4 6 1
2
5 1
1
3 6 2
Includes 80 Puzzles
Peter I. Kattan
Nicola I. Kattan